Dedication

This book is dedicated to all the people who have lost loved ones before their time, those who know all too well the tragedy of suicide, those who have survived the thoughts and attempts, those who still struggle, those who supported and continue to support them and those whose lives were cut short.

Acknowledgements

A huge thanks to everyone who did work on the book and supported me through the process. I love you all!
Marie Gudgel
All the Kepharts
Extended Family
Likeminded Family
Rhiannon James-Editor
Ashley Baker-Artist
Sam Benavides-Photographer
Kent Gordon-Professor
Judy Brown-Yoga Instructor
Joshua Rosenthal and Lindsay Smith-Instructors

The Color Inside

Copyright © 2015 by KATY KEPHART

All rights reserved. No part of this book may be reproduced in any form or by any electronic or mechanical means, including information storage and retrieval systems, without permission in writing from the author. For information, contact KATY KEPHART at author.thecolorinside@gmail.com

The content of this book is for general instruction only. Each person's physical, emotional, and spiritual condition is unique. The instruction in this book is not intended to replace or interrupt the reader's relationship with a physician or other professional. Please consult your doctor for matters pertaining to your specific health and diet.

All rights reserved. No part of this publication may be reproduced, distributed, or transmitted in any form or by any means, including photocopying, recording, or other electronic or mechanical methods, without the prior written permission of the publisher or author, except in the case of brief quotations embodied in critical reviews and certain other noncommercial uses permitted by copyright law. For permission requests, email the publisher or author at author.thecolorinside@gmail.com or send your request to

5925 N May Ave. Oklahoma City, OK 73112

To contact the publisher or author, visit katy-kephart.healthcoach.integrativenutrition.com

ISBN **978-0692404775**

Printed in the United States of America

Table of Contents

1. Introduction..5
2. Loss..6
3. Struggle...16
4. Realization...24
5. Healing and Resilience............................31
6. Resource Page......................................51
7. Bibliography.......................................52

Introduction

When they said, "There's nothing more we can do," my heart broke. It would be a long time before I would feel whole again.

1234 N Somewhere Ave
City, ST 70010
October 29, 2005

Dear Diary,

Today was a blur. I'm scared that I am going to be missing someone I love very much in the near future. I went to the hospital with some friends from youth group. They were all very sweet and supportive of me in this hard time. I remember the drive was silent. There was nothing to say. When we arrived there was an ominous feeling hanging in the air. I could sense the pain all around me. It made my heart pound loud in my ears. It was like the movies when the sound fades, and all you can hear are feet clicking on the tile and a heart beating like a drum. My chest is tight; the air feels thick and heavy as we approach the room. I can't breathe. My hand reaches for the door handle in what seems like slow motion. The metal is icy and makes my chest clench tighter. The door clicks and the smell of chemicals, sickness, and bad hospital food hits me in the face. It's like a vacuum as the air changes from cold and sterile to the warm and stagnant. My dad is lying there with all kinds of tubes and cords hooked up to him like a science experiment. His hair is almost all gone and there are sores around his mouth and nose. His once strong carpenter arms are flabby and atrophied. My friends file in and the door clicks closed. I stand there at the side of his bed while everyone else stands in a semi circle around the other side. One of my friends suggests that we sing a song to him. I agree because music means a lot to my dad. I whisper, "Amazing Grace," since it is his favorite hymn and we start singing. My voice trembles and I can barely get the words out. We are all holding hands surrounding the bed. All of a sudden my dad begins to shake. He goes into a grand mal seizure. I am terrified. The nurses come in within seconds, and the sound fades out again. Each second feels like a year. A gripping force tears at my insides as the hospital staff try to stabilize him. I can't breathe. I'm crying but no sound will come out. It is a crippling feeling, gasping for air. It's all so foggy after that. The next thing I remember is being in a room with my godparents.

                                        Talk to you soon,

                                                        Katy

1234 N Somewhere Ave
City, ST 70010
November 2, 2005

Dear Daddy,

When I came to visit you today, you looked so different from the dad I once knew. So frail and weak, yet you were so peaceful. It was as if you knew what was going to happen. You were ready to go home. I held your hand and told you about my week at school. Even though you couldn't respond, I knew you were listening. Your watery sky blue eyes told your story. When I left you, I went to school just as I would every other normal day. But today was not a normal day. I went to my first class, which was band. The director was teaching us something, but I wasn't paying attention. It must not have been more than an hour before the intercom buzzed into the band room. The secretary called my name to come to the office to check out. I gathered my things in a haze and made my way toward the office. Grandpa was waiting there for me. I was very confused but I could feel something was wrong. I had no idea that today was the transition point of a life with you to a life without you—that the moment I told you I loved you and hugged you would be the final goodbye in this life, or that today was the day you would take your last breath and all your pain would be gone. Grandpa and I were silent as we made our way to Becky's house. She opened the door and welcomed me in. Abby and Kenzy were sitting on the big tan couch. Grandpa kissed my forehead and went back to be with mom. After he left, Becky gathered all of the sisters in her living room with blue carpet and a zebra print rug. Her voice broke as she said, "Daddy's gone to be with Jesus." The world seemed to slow down as soon as the last word fell from her lips. Immediately, a waterfall burst from my eyes. I knew that this day was coming, but not that it would be so soon. My already broken heart was torn to shreds and left on the floor to bleed. I was so lost.

I love you and miss you dearly,

Katy

1234 N Somewhere Ave
City, ST 70010
November 5, 2005

Dear Daddy,

The memorial service was today. There was an incredible amount of people there. You obviously had a great impact on the community. I had no idea that so many people knew you. I can only hope that I will have a similar impact on the people around me. It was so surreal. Music was playing, and we filed in as a family after everyone else had arrived. The service started, and people were talking about you; it didn't feel like you were gone. I learned about you from your friends and people that you touched. All I could think was that I wished you were there next to me to hold my hand. I felt numb from my toes to my face. I didn't cry much. It was like the tears were frozen in a vault until someone knew the combination. And when they did, it came like a flood. Hot waterfalls poured down my cheeks until my head felt like it was going to pop off. My eyes felt like they'd been wrung out and left on the sink like an old sponge. The one friend I had hoped would show up did. You know the one. He was there for me when I really needed him. The night you passed on, he invited me to a Star Wars marathon. We vegged out in front of a huge TV in his garage, jumped on the trampoline, and he sang "Bohemian Rhapsody" in the back yard—the WHOLE thing. It was just what I needed.

Love you,

Katy

1234 N Somewhere Ave
City, ST 70010
December 10, 2005

Dear Daddy,

Remember the day we went to get the new van? It was really scary for me. I could tell something was terribly wrong. We pulled in to the car place to pick it up. At first, I was so excited to ride with you in the new van. You said you were fine so Mom drove Becky's car back to the house. When you started driving you were swerving all over the place, and I started getting really worried. I didn't want to say anything because I didn't even have a license yet. I was so relieved when we pulled into the driveway. It didn't make sense at the time, but now I understand.

                                                      I miss you,

                                                        Katy

1234 N Somewhere Ave
City, ST 70010
January 4, 2006

Dear Daddy,

Happy Birthday. I miss you more every day. I still don't really believe that you're gone. I keep having dreams that you were never gone, everything is normal, and you were just playing a joke on us. That would be a twisted joke. I also dream that you just went away on a trip for a few months and then you came back. When I wake up, I realize you're not there, and it breaks my heart all over again. I look forward to sleep because I get to see you. I'm not doing very well. I keep thinking of all the things I will never get to do with you or you will never see. I'll never get to go camping with you again. You loved camping. You won't get to see me get my braces off or graduate. You won't even see my 16th birthday. I could go on and on, but the thing that upsets me the most is that you won't be there to walk me down the isle when I get married. No one can truly take that place. I love you so much.

See you in dreamland,

Katy

1234 N Somewhere Ave
City, ST 70010
February 5, 2006

Dear Daddy,

I joined the school musical! They needed extra townspeople so I decided to audition. Not only did I get the part of townsperson, but I have a solo too! I know you would be proud of me. Even though you won't get to see me in the musical, I know you will be with me in spirit. It makes me sad when I think about the fact that I will never get to sing with you again in this life. Sometimes I hear you singing when we're in church, or listening to music on the radio. Mom said she has a tape somewhere of you guys singing in a choir. I hope we can find it so I can hear you sing in a more tangible form again. I really do miss that. I don't want to forget how your voice sounds. I never realized how lucky I was to have both parents with musical talent. It's pretty rare. I will always cherish the times I got to spend with you in the truck on the way to church or school when you'd whistle along to the radio.

                                        Love you,

Katy

1234 N Somewhere Ave
City, ST 70010
April 18, 2006

Dear Daddy,

I have decided to quit band to join choir. I was never happy playing flute in the band. Yes I made some good friends, but it seems like I am going to let life pass me by if I stay. I'm scared to break the news to the director. He is a little intimidating, but it's something I have to do. I have this talent that I have been hiding. I finally realized that this is what I want, and I found a way to get it out there. The choir director basically begged me to join. I love the people in choir; they are all nice and accepting so far. Some of the people in choir are friends from middle school that I haven't seen very much since then.
It makes me sad that you won't get to see me perform with the choir; it's one of the few things that make me happy.

Love you,

Katy

1234 N Somewhere Ave
City, ST 70010
December 13, 2006

Dear Friend,

My most recent doctor's appointment was one of the most depressing moments of my life. I have gained 35 lbs. in the year since my dad's passing. As you know I have always struggled with my weight and body image. I am so embarrassed that I let my overeating get to this point. My mom wants me to go to a weight loss program at a church down the street with her. I am not ready for that kind of public humiliation. I feel absolutely disgusting. I hate my reflection. I will have to do something about the extra weight, even though it's the last thing I want to focus on. I want to ignore it and make it disappear.

                                                  Sincerely,

                                                    Katy

1234 N Somewhere Ave
City, ST 70010
February 17, 2007

Dear Friend,

I started going to the weight loss program with my mom. It's kind of restricting and hard, but I'm starting to lose weight and feel better. I had been sabotaging myself for a long time. I was holding on to the pain for dear life because I was scared of what would happen when I let go. I have started to loosen my grasp, but I still have a long way to go. The ladies are so nice, and they make it seem less daunting. Everyone there is trying to do the same thing that I am. I'm learning about portion size and calorie counting, which I never really knew about. I really hated showing up for the weigh-ins at first, but now it's not as hard because the number on the scale is getting smaller. It is hard not to beat myself up for messing up. I tend to have an all or nothing mentality; I feel like throwing it all out the window when I do something wrong. Wish me luck.

Sincerely,

Katy

1234 N Somewhere Ave
City, ST 70010
December 20, 2007

Dear Diary,

I have lost 45 lbs. since I started the program. I fell off the wagon for a while, but I got back up and kept going. No one is perfect, right? I haven't told anyone this because I think they would judge me. I haven't been eating much at all the last few months. I've been eating maybe one meal a day and usually no more than 500 or 600 calories in a day. I've been obsessing over each morsel that goes past my lips. I even weigh broccoli slaw to the fraction of an ounce, and it's driving me crazy. In my head I think I've got this system hacked. I think, "If I eat less and less, I weight less and less," but in reality, I'm lying to everyone around me. And worst of all I'm lying to myself. My heart knows that this isn't good. When I go out to dinner with my friends I tell them that I ate a big meal earlier, order iced tea, and use the artificial no calorie sweetener. I feel good when I don't eat because I know that I will stay thin. Since my mom was in the program with me, she doesn't think it's strange when I eat a very small meal. When I look in the mirror I still see the girl that I was a year ago. I see every bit of fat and feel guilty for eating. The word "cow" keeps flashing behind my eyes.

Talk soon,

Katy

1234 N Somewhere Ave
City, ST 70010
October 31, 2007

Dear Diary,

I've met a girl who's really beautiful. She works with me at the pet store. People say we look alike. They often ask us if we're sisters, and sometimes we tell them that we are just for fun. I'm flattered that people think that. She is a lesbian, and she has a girlfriend. The way they are so open about it and brave enough to tell the world always intrigues me. I wish I were brave. My lips are glued together when I have a chance to say what I really feel. I don't know how to open the door that leads to the truth. Am I a coward for keeping this secret? I am scared of the repercussions. I'm scared of what people will think. I'm horrified that I might be on display. Why can't I just be me and not worry about what people think? There is this aching that pulls me further inward. The deepest parts of my soul want to come to the surface.

Talk soon,

Katy

1234 N Somewhere Ave
City, ST 70010
November 19, 2007

Dear Diary,

Today I went to a new doctor with my mom. I told my mom I didn't want to go to my pediatrician anymore. I'm too old for that. The doctor is an odd blonde lady who was wearing bright fuchsia lipstick, velvet pants, and a powder blue sweater. She talked to me like I was a child, but I got my diagnosis. She said, "Honey I think you have a little bit of depression." Like I didn't know. Thanks. Then she gave me a medicine to try. I was a little uneasy about taking medication again because I haven't been taking any prescription drugs since I stopped my Ritalin in 8th grade. I'm kind of desperate right now. I want to feel better.

                                              Talk soon,

                                                    Katy

1234 N Somewhere Ave
City, ST 70010
June 29, 2008

Dear Diary,

I have been seeing a man for over a month now. His kisses bore me. I find myself thinking of her every time we touch. Nothing is holding my attention with him, except the fact that he wants me. He is not very interesting, intelligent, talented or sexy. I grow more dissatisfied with the relationship every day. I have yet to find the courage to break the news to him. Everything I'm doing is really just a smokescreen for my family. I am being a hypocrite. I am desperately in love with a woman. She is the most beautiful creature on the planet. When we are together nothing in the world matters. We don't have to be doing anything, and it's the happiest moment of my life. I even use the guy to get closer to her, since they are friends. My heart is a pincushion that gets a new pin every time I have a chance to tell her. She asks me who this girl could be and tries to guess, but I cower away from the real answer every time. I developed a habit of telling her practically everything. She has to be suspicious. I couldn't bear the thought of losing her, so I left her in the dark. I become tongue tied only when I have a chance to tell her the truth.

Talk soon,

Katy

University of Central Oklahoma
Edmond, OK 73034
November 7, 2008

Dear Diary,

This is the lowest I've ever felt in my entire life. I live with a stranger. I am finding myself looking for sharp objects around my dorm room. I want to just end it all right now and take the pain away. There's a weight on my chest that is getting heavier and heavier. I feel I might be crushed under the pressure. I'm lonely in a sea of people. Each day seems the same. Stay up way too late drinking, come back to do homework and not finish, get up to go to class, get through class, pound energy drinks all day to be able to function, start over. When will it end?

1234 Somewhere Ave
City, ST 70010
February 8, 2010

Dear Friend,

It should have been a red flag; a "Stop right where you are and take a look at yourself," moment. Black out after black out, I kept binge drinking. This one ended up putting me in a horrible situation. Wake up! It's time to turn a different direction. He touched me with his dirty hands, and it hurt. I was so alone and so scared, but I couldn't move. He told everyone of his conquest, and they all shook their heads in disbelief. "Katy isn't into men." He bragged that he had sex with me. I played it off by saying something like, "only if sex to him means shoving his hand down my pants, then sure, we 'had sex'," only as a defense mechanism because I was so broken and raw inside. I can never be sure of what he did to me. I may have been drugged. I wasn't able to move or see but I could still hear everything, and I remember feeling too. Just because there wasn't penal penetration doesn't mean it wasn't rape.

                                       Thanks for listening,

                                                          Katy

1234 N Somewhere Ave
City, ST 70010
May 16, 2011

Dear Diary,

I have been missing something ever since I dropped out of school after freshman year at UCO. I haven't really played music or sang in a long time except for karaoke. One of my friends told me about the school he is going to called ACM, the Academy of Contemporary Music. He said it is a totally different kind of school. They are in bands that are randomly assigned by the instructors, and they have to learn to work together to play a different set of songs every week. It sounds like something I would really enjoy. I've been teaching myself how to play guitar sporadically over the last couple of years, so it might be the kick I need to get into the music game. It would definitely give me opportunities to meet other musicians. I've been feeling very lost working in the salon. I'm not giving my best effort and I need to bring myself out of this funk. I went to school for music and I felt like I had given up on it until now.

> Talk soon,
>
> Katy

1234 Somewhere Ave
City, ST 70010
December 5, 2011

Dear Diary,

I have to change something. I'm bursting at the seams, and rapidly heading toward my own demise. The lies I have been telling myself to deflect the true problem and justify my actions, the monotonous nights of drinking to the point of blacking out or vomiting, the meaningless conversations that I probably won't remember in the morning, the same scene with different backgrounds but no purpose. I've managed to shove the truth down so far that I'm ignoring the magnitude of recklessness. Just because a person doesn't drink every day doesn't mean they are sober. I have become accustomed to the heavy feeling in the morning after a binge. It is normal to feel like hell, every muscle sucked dry, so stiff that it's hard to move. It's just not real enough. I am becoming less amused with stories of nights I can't remember. I'm not proud of how I have been acting. I lose control and expect whoever I am with to deal with it. I'm lucky no one has left me to fend for myself. I've driven drunk more times than I can count, and whoever is "less drunk" drives. I don't know how I thought that was acceptable. I can't expect to derive anything meaningful from this life of non-stop partying. I'm not going anywhere with my career because of it. I need to get unstuck. The hard part is knowing how. I'm starting to realize that it is not anyone's fault but my own that I am in this situation. I have been wasting so much time blaming the world for my problems. It's time to grow up and take responsibility for myself.

Talk soon,

Katy

1234 N Somewhere Ave
City, ST 70010
Feb 6, 2012

Dear Diary,

I made a really stupid mistake. My intention wasn't bad, but the way I did it was. I have wanted this tattoo for a long time, but I went to my friend's friend at his house. It is supposed to be a tribute to dad with his and my love of music blended with his carpentry. It turned out horribly. I liked it at first, but now that it has healed I can see every flaw. The lines are shaky and the shading is basically non-existent because he just colored it in where it's supposed to be shaded. It's bad. To make matters worse, I found out that he was doing meth in between. I made kind of a rash decision when I got it. I had just been broken up with after a short-lived, destructive relationship. I really liked her though. I didn't realize it at the time, but we were always altered in some way when we were together, whether it was pills, alcohol, or marijuana. We were maybe sober once in the relationship: our first date when we had lunch on her break from work. It has been a permanent reminder of how idiotic I was being at the time. I'm still drinking too much. I know my limit, but I exceed it anyway. I just don't seem to care about myself enough to try. I'm not supposed to be drinking at all with my medication. Since alcohol is a depressant, I feel the effects very strongly the morning after.

Talk soon,

Katy

1234 N Somewhere Ave
City, ST 70010
February 15, 2012

Dear Diary,

I have to face the fact that I'm not going to be where I want to be unless I change something. I just wanted to ignore reality. Every time I wake up and raid the cabinets or the fridge, I shove a pacifier into the real problem. On top of that, I look forward to being altered more than anything throughout the day. On nights that I go out, there is no limit to how much I drink. It usually results in getting sick or passing out. Recently, it has turned into blacking out. There is no telling what I might do or say when I am so far gone. I used to think it was funny to not remember anything from the night before, but now I'm realizing that it is childish and unfulfilling. I don't want to be typical. Go to the gym to look good, get drunk, and make out with strangers. What kind of life is that? There is no real substance. I guess I was just biding my time until I had the wake up call. It's hard to say no when I keep hanging out with the same crowd. They are just as in over their heads as I am.

                                                    Talk soon,

                                                       Katy

1234 N Somewhere Ave
City, ST 70010
June 19, 2012

Dear Diary,

Yesterday was my first open mic. It was scary being up there singing by myself in a public setting, but it wasn't nearly as terrifying as the first day performing with my band at school. For one thing I didn't have instructors watching with their pencils and grade sheets waiting for me to make a mistake. It will help me practice my confidence on stage, and it's a networking opportunity. The girl hosting the open mic is cool. She inspired me to get up and play something after letting me sing with her on a couple of well-known cover songs. It's also a good way to get some objective feedback from people who don't know me. I'm excited to come back next week!

                                                  Talk soon,

                                                        Katy

1234 N Somewhere Ave
City, ST 70010
January 2, 2014

Dear Diary,

I've decided that I'm worth the effort to make a change. I've been in a rut for a few months, but I've started researching detoxes and cleanses. I am going to try the raw food cleanse for a little while and see how it makes me feel. The more I read the more I seem to want to know. I think I may have uncovered a passion that I didn't know I had. I've always been semi-conscious about what I eat since the program I did back in high school. Now I'm learning about the quality of food in deeper ways than I ever thought to look. I don't know how I was so blind before. I feel like I've been opened up to a new world. I don't get tired of watching documentary after documentary about nutrients, genetically modified organisms, organic, raw, anything you could think of that has to do with food, food politics and nutrition. I even love discussing it with other people. Some of the things I have learned have made me so angry. For example, the treatment of animals on factory farms or the chemicals that have been pumped into my system as well as my family's systems under the radar because of pesticides, hormones and genetic engineering. Just the sheer fact that disease rates have gone up since GMOs hit the market—without extensive testing—makes my blood boil. It's hard to even know what does and doesn't contain GMOs anymore unless it's labeled. I want America to get with the program and finally allow labeling of all products that may contain GMOs so that people can choose for themselves. I personally don't want to consume something that could be potentially lethal without my consent. The system is so flawed by power hungry people. If it was about the health of the consumer instead of money, we would have never had the issue of labeling, because food would just be food like it always has been since the dawn of time.

Talk soon,

Katy

1234 N Somewhere Ave
City, ST 70010
January 18, 2014

Dear Friend,

If you are like me, then you have been put down in some way for something you couldn't change, or maybe something you could change but you just didn't know how at the time. I wish it wasn't true, but every time someone puts you down it takes a piece of you and breaks it right in front of your eyes. If you don't know how to let it roll off, it can do some serious damage. The moment I realized that every person on the planet has insecurities just as I do, that people aren't mean just because they have evil in their DNA, and that everyone makes mistakes, I was able to take people's comments with a grain of salt instead of letting them define my truth. Yes it still hurts if someone puts me down, but I'm able to disconnect myself from those words that are merely that. Just words. Yes the tongue can cut deeper than any knife, but my ability to heal the wound has become stronger. It's only human to care what other humans think of me. It's wise to give more weight to the opinions of people who I love and who love me. It's hard to learn that discernment but it's the leverage that you give negativity that makes it hurt so much. I was trying so hard for so long not to be something that people dislike, that I got off the path to finding who I truly am. Once I got to the point that I could see this vicious cycle of negativity, I started to be me again. The pieces that bullies, beaus and bosses had chipped away were starting to come back together. Don't let other people's words define you.

>Talk soon,
>
>Katy

1234 Somewhere Ave
City, ST 70010
March 5, 2014

Dear Bestie,

I feel like I'm coming out again. I have been hiding something for a long time and it's finally time to tell someone outside of my family. They have been telling me to stop for years, and I don't know how. It's an addiction. I didn't really even know that it was bad until I learned more about self-harm behavior. I pick at my skin all over my body wherever I can reach. I pull out leg hairs and arm hairs with tweezers or dig into my skin with them. Sometimes it goes on for a lot longer than I would like to admit. More often than not I make myself bleed. I have been doing this since I was eleven but I didn't realize how bad it was until I spoke with my therapist. It's a struggle every single day. I don't know how to stop. I've been doing this for so long that it's second nature. It started with my face when I was a preteen and had zits. It was probably harmless then, but I didn't stop. Years and years of doing it became more and more harmful. It became a shameful act. It escalated into cutting myself with scissors for a while. I can't say that it is better or worse than any other addiction. Sometimes I think to myself, "at least I'm not…" to make myself feel better. The truth is I did end up doing a lot of those things. But you know all about that. The point is that I trust you and you should know the true extent of it.

                                                Love you,

                                                   Katy

1234 N Somewhere Ave
City, ST 70010
July 10, 2014

Dear Friend,

The time has come when I must either increase the dosage of my medication again or try a different approach. They don't seem to be doing much for me anymore. I feel trapped by my thoughts and I want to try an alternative method. I'm going to the doctor this week to see about weaning off so I can see how I feel. If I feel worse, I will go back, but I have to try it. At this point, increasing my medication is not a viable option. I don't want to medicate my symptoms anymore. I want to see if my true self can exist without the crutch. I am much stronger now than I was when I first went on them. I have learned a lot about life and myself in the last few years. I've come to understand that if I want something for myself I have to make it happen. I want to see if I can heal the cause of the disease. I want to make an impact in the world. I want to feel again. I want to accept myself as a whole, flaws and all.

                                            Talk soon,

                                                     Katy

1234 N Somewhere Ave
City, ST 70010
August 12, 2014

Dear Diary,

I have come to the conclusion that I can control the direction of my life. Of course there will be obstacles and things that are out of my control but I have the reigns. It's not going to be easy coming through to the other side of the dark places that my mind goes. It is not something that just goes away one day and never comes back. The strength comes a little at a time by moving forward no matter how small the step. I do not always know what to do but I have things that I know work for me that I can go to in those times. There won't be a quick fix without pharmaceutical medication as a crutch. It's for me to decide what happens next, which is scary but also very freeing. I am capable of getting out of the rut. If I need help, I will ask for it. If I need to talk, I will tell someone. I am the only one standing in my way.

                                                Talk soon,

                                                       Katy

1234 N Somewhere Ave
City, ST 70010
December 8, 2014

Dear Friend,

Sometimes when I accidentally cut myself, I see the blood, and I think about how pretty it is. For a split second, a scenario plays out in my head as I'm cleaning the cut. I see the knife piercing the milky white flesh of my upper leg. The rubies pour out. I'm sorry to be graphic; I know it is not good to hurt myself on purpose. I have to wonder what may happen when it's not enough to know. I have to make the effort every time to pull myself away. I had to tell someone. It's the only way to stop my emotions from controlling me.

                                            Talk soon,

                                                   Katy

1234 N Somewhere Ave
City, ST 70010
December 9, 2014

Dear Friend,

You know I have seen a lot of friends and loved ones stumble through substance addiction. It didn't get bad enough for me to spiral out, yet I am still addicted to picking. I'm a functional addict. It's something that still I haven't been able to control. I'm also a sugar addict. It's the most addictive substance on the planet and I know that but I haven't been able to stop for any significant amount of time. I know I haven't fixed my problems but I still try to help others. But that is the thing about most people in the realm of helping people. You don't have to be perfect to share your knowledge. Human connection is what saves people. The most important thing is to share the issues you have. Spill them out on paper, canvas, through a melody, in a conversation, or any way you can imagine. It makes you appear more tangible, real, and human. It strips away the façade that we put on to be accepted as "normal." There is no such thing as normal. Do something to shatter the societal burden of judgment. Don't be afraid to stand out. Let your color out.

                                                Talk soon,

                                                     Katy

1234 N Somewhere Ave
City, ST 70010
December 10, 2014

Dear Friend,

Sometimes I feel everything is against me, and I can't do anything right. When I have days like that, I have to take a step back and see the fear for what it is. I have to dig deep to find the energy to keep going, even though I don't think I can. I draw positivity from my partner, my dog, music, other people—they might even be strangers in the room at a coffee shop or the library—and anything that will get me over the seemingly impossible hurdle. Isolation is not the best option when I'm feeling low. I have to peel myself off of the floor at times. I once watched a speaker who said you have to make the effort to get out of autopilot. It's called activation energy. The same effort it takes to get out of bed in the morning from the cozy blankets into a cold room is the effort it takes to make a change.

Talk soon,

Katy

1234 Somewhere Ave
City, ST 70010
December 12, 2014

Dear Friend,

My circle of friends changed quite a bit after the musical. I didn't intentionally do this, but the majority of my friends were gay, lesbian, bi, or supportive of gay people. I didn't even realize I was gay yet. I was in denial about it. It's crazy the people you draw into your life to open the box you've been keeping secret from yourself. Looking back, there were definitely signs, but when you're there it's different. I didn't know why I was having these crushes on women. I didn't even really know it was a crush at the time. I was deep in the closet, but I started to move towards the door because of these friends. My mom even knew before I told her. I was in love with a girl that wouldn't give me the time of day. We were friends, but I was way too shy to say anything. Especially since I had no idea if love was what it was. The more I hung out with people who were like me and supported me, the easier it became to understand myself. It was clear that I was not a heterosexual female, but I didn't know what that meant. I was so shy around anyone I had any interest in. I decided that I had to keep it a secret for a little while longer. I couldn't let my little sister hear it from someone else in school, so I held it in. It was torture. Every time I had an opportunity to say, "Yes, I am attracted to women and I might be bisexual, but I don't know," I chickened out. My friends all pretty much knew. Each time there was a pain in my chest. "Just say it!" my heart would scream. "Be authentically you!" But it wouldn't come out of my mouth. I got so twisted up in the lie that I began to sound judgmental and borderline homophobic. I said things like, "I don't care if you're a lesbian as long as you don't hit on me." Like I was such a prize or that it would be unflattering if a woman hit on me but not if a guy did. I was very tangled in my own web because I wasn't living as my true self. I was living in the cookie cutter world that wanted me to marry a nice godly man, have nice children, and live in a nice house. I didn't even like myself anymore. I was hiding behind this mask so I didn't have to be vulnerable. It seems silly to me that people even have to come out of this proverbial "closet" when they shouldn't have been branded as "straight" or "heterosexual" in the first place. Yes, we are the minority but it really shouldn't matter who people inherently love.

Talk soon,

Katy

1234 N Somewhere Ave
City, ST 70010
December 13, 2014

Dear Sissy,

Thank you for being so compassionate, understanding and warm. You were the first one I came out to in the family. It will forever be one of the moments I remember as fond. That night was the page that turned to the next chapter. I had the confidence to divulge the truth about who I am to the rest of the family. Mom already knew, but I just hadn't confronted her about it yet. I love you so much.

                                                      Talk soon,

                                                         Katy

1234 N Somewhere Ave
City, ST 70010
December 15, 2014

Dear Friend,

If there is one thing I want to echo from my journey through depression, it is that no matter how bad it feels, reach out somehow. Write it down, tell a friend, call a hotline. Healing will not happen if it is all internalized and doesn't come out. It is imperative to understand that emotions alone are not going to hurt you. Fear itself cannot push you off the cliff, sadness cannot cut you, helplessness cannot kill you.

I have learned to listen to my body in the last few months. The voice was always there, but it only gets stronger with time. Our bodies are smarter than we are. They were programmed from birth to sustain life. Disease is not our body making a mistake; it is its way of dealing with environment, stress, poor nutrition or exhaustion. Unless there is something wrong, our heart never misses a beat. It maintains 98.6 degrees, and our organs do what they were intended to do without our conscious effort.

Talk soon,

Katy

1234 N Somewhere Ave
City, ST 70010
December 29, 2014

Dear Friend,

This journey through depression and recovery is not straight and narrow. It is full of ups, downs, curves and cliffs. There will be some extremes, but know that tomorrow is a new day no matter what happens today. It is never too late to turn a page, to start fresh, or to change your thinking. People who don't have depression have lows and highs too. We just have to put effort into things that help us bear the lows and celebrate the highs. It's not a perfect science. No one knows what will help until they try it. The best thing to do is to become more aware of your triggers. I started to tune in to whether I am experiencing fear or if the situation is really going to harm me in that moment. Once I could tell the difference, I was able to stop destructive thoughts in their tracks. My yoga teacher, Judy, always says this when we are in sevasana, or "corpse pose:" "Go to your third eye, which is located between your brow. Find a safe place; a place you are alone but you're not scared. It is the most beautiful place you can imagine, maybe it is a place you have been, a place you would like to go or it is a place you invent. That place is always with you. You can find it whenever you need it. When you come back from this place, the problems you were facing will still be there, but maybe you can handle them a little differently." I love the idea that emotions are controllable.

                                    Talk soon,

                                        Katy

1234 N Somewhere Ave
City, ST 70010
December 21, 2014

Dear Mom,

You saved my life that night. I called you crying, and you told me everything was going to be okay. It was two in the morning, and you said to come home, so I did. You let me vent and cry until it was all out. You held me like I was still your perfect little girl and I had done nothing wrong. I want to earnestly thank you from the bottom of my heart, because I would not be here today if it wasn't for you. You picked me up off the floor and gave me hope that tomorrow would be better. I couldn't ask for a better mom.

                                      I love you so much,

                                                            Katy

1234 N Somewhere Ave
City, ST 70010
January 9, 2015

Dear Friend,

When I look in the mirror sometimes I still see a monster. I know that my interpretation of my appearance is not always based in reality. I'm the one living inside this body and I am a harsh critic. I have to take a step back and look from an outside perspective. If I took all emotion out of the equation and I was as a bystander what would I think? I see the way I look without the cloud of self-judgment. I see myself with the same compassion and objectivity that I would have for a stranger. The translation of my physical manifestation by my emotional scars, fear, and genetics is no longer monstrous.

Talk soon,

Katy

1234 N Somewhere Ave
City, ST 70010
January 4, 2015

Dear Friend,

My dad has been gone for a long time now, but I still miss him every day. I miss how he smelled of sawdust and drywall mud when he came home from work. It's an aroma that might make most people turn their nose away, but I would take a big inhale when I hugged him. It was a comforting smell for me. It's warm and earthy and slightly harsh like chemicals at the same time. He gave the best hugs. A big bear hug that made you forget about your troubles for that moment. Now my partner comes home smelling of paint and drywall, and it brings me back to my childhood. My dad was an artist with cabinetry and woodwork. I still meet people who had work done in their house by him. People who knew him tell me stories of his kindness and generosity. Just this morning I woke with a feeling that he had been there in my dream. I still feel close to him almost a decade later. His memory lives on in my heart.

Talk soon,

Katy

1234 N Somewhere Ave
City, ST 70010
March 1, 2015

Dear Friend,

I had given up on love. I know it seems dramatic, but I felt this inconsistency my whole life. I am genuine and honest in my relationships, and they still never worked out. I thought it had to be me if it kept happening the same way. I have a hard time stepping out of my little world to let people know I have an interest in them. I met a woman named Marie at a social gathering that I was invited to by my best friend. She was unlike anyone I had ever met before. I had never pursued anyone before, but I took a chance and stepped out of my comfort zone.

At the time, I was trapped in a maze with a girl I hardly knew. She was there in a time of my life after 2 bad relationships, and I wanted nothing to do with love. She sweet-talked me, and even after my repeated explanation of why we could never work, I fell for it. She was in the military getting ready for deployment, and we had decided to be just friends. She was deployed in May, and I met Marie in June 2012. I wrote her letters, talked on the phone and skyped with her while she was overseas. I told her about Marie in letters. Since we were never actually together, I thought she would be happy for me. In fact, she told me how happy she was for us.

Talk soon,

Katy

1234 N Somewhere Ave
City, ST 70010
March 12, 2015

Dear Friend,

I have come to realize that life is trial and error. I used to beat myself up for making stupid mistakes. But I have learned that that only hurts me and doesn't do anything positive on any level. I have to take each mistake with a grain of salt and learn from it. I have heard from so many wise people that being afraid of failure will only hinder your progress. It can stunt your growth and cause procrastination. Embrace the possibility of failure because from it comes experience. It can only teach you what not to do. Fail better next time. Nelson Mandela says it in one of my favorite ways, "The greatest glory in living lies not in never falling, but in rising every time we fall."

All my love,

Katy

Resources

American Foundation for Suicide Prevention (AFSP)
www.afsp.org
In an emergency, contact:
Suicide Prevention Hotline 1-800-273-TALK (8255)
Psychiatric hospital walk-in clinic
Hospital emergency room
Urgent care clinic
Call 911

GLBT National Help Center www.glnh.org
National Help Line 1-888-THE-GLNH (1-888-843-4564)
Peer counseling, information, and local resources

National Eating Disorders Association
www.nationaleatingdisorders.org
Helpline 1-800-931-2237

National Addiction Helpline
www.nationaladdictionhelpline.com
1-866-507-7111

Rape Assault and Incest National Network (RAINN)
www.rainn.org
The nation's largest anti-sexual assault organization:
National Sexual Assault Hotline 1-800-656-HOPE (4673)

Bibliography

Robbins, Mel. "How to Stop Screwing Yourself Over."

    Tedx Talks. United States, San Fransisco.

    Lecture.

Rosenthal, Joshua. "Integrative Nutrition Theory Review."

    IIN Course. United States, New York City, NY.

    Lecture.

www.ingramcontent.com/pod-product-compliance
Lightning Source LLC
Chambersburg PA
CBHW041757040426
42446CB00005B/237